THE PRIDE OF UNFORGIVENESS

Breaking up the Fallow Ground of the Heart

TEMEILA C. DANIEL

CONCISE
PUBLISHING HOUSE

The Pride of Unforgiveness: Breaking up the Fallow Ground of the Heart

ISBN: 979-8-9909626-8-2

Concise Publishing House
120 Preston Executive Drive Suite 229
Cary, NC 27513
www.ConcisePublishing.us

Dedication

To those who carried pain quietly, loved deeply, and are now ready to lay the weight down.

Contents

FOREWORD i

PREFACE iv

How This Book Was Born

The Moment of Exposure viii

Introduction.. xiii

CHAPTER 1 1

The Silent Bondage of Unforgiveness

CHAPTER 2...................................... 9

Pride: The Root Beneath the Bitterness

CHAPTER 3 19

When "I Deserve Better" Becomes an Idol

CHAPTER 4 29

The Illusion of Forgiveness

CHAPTER 5 37

The Cycle of Control

CHAPTER 6 45

When God Rewrites the Story

CHAPTER 7 53

Learning the Unforced Rhythms of Grace

CHAPTER 8 59

The Spirit That Twists

PART II 67

The Prayer Room

THE PRAYER ROOM 68

The Interior Life of a Restored Heart

Restored to Rest 73

PART III 77

Wisdom for the Restored Heart

FOREWORD

There are books that inform, and there are books that *invite excavation*. This work belongs to the latter.

The Pride of Unforgiveness: Breaking Up the Fallow Ground of the Heart does not approach the reader with accusation, but with **holy confrontation wrapped in truth and mercy**. It speaks to the places we have learned to protect, excuse, spiritualize, or ignore—those quiet chambers of the heart where unforgiveness can sit undisturbed, unchallenged, and unnamed.

What makes this book both compelling and necessary is its **transparency**. The author does not write from theory, but from **experience, process, and deliverance**. She exposes the subtlety of unforgiveness—not as an explosive sin, but as a *silent bondage*. One that hides behind reason, justification, survival, and even spiritual language. One that slowly hardens the soil of the heart until fruitfulness becomes difficult and intimacy with God becomes strained.

Unforgiveness, when left unattended, does not remain passive. It matures. It takes root. And as this book powerfully reveals, it often gives birth to **bitterness**, a root that grows beneath the surface while life above it continues as normal. Cycles begin—emotional, relational, spiritual—and many never realize the origin of their struggle is not what happened to them, but what was never released from them.

Yet this is not a book of despair.

This is a book of **hope, healing, and holy interruption**.

With clarity and compassion, the author leads the reader through the breaking up of fallow ground—the painful but necessary process of allowing God to plow the heart again. She reminds us that deliverance is not denial, and freedom is not forgetting, but **yielding the hardened places back to the hands of the Healer**.

This book calls the reader forward—not to shame, but to **freedom**. Not to remain stuck in cycles, but to step into **deliverance as a final outcome**. Not to carry pride disguised as protection, but to embrace humility that leads to restoration.

It is my prayer that as you read, you will not rush. Let the words search you. Let the Spirit speak. And let the ground of your heart become fertile again— forgiveness released, bitterness uprooted, and life restored.

— Apostle Dr. Shirley R. Brown, Th.D

PREFACE
How This Book Was Born

Before *The Pride of Unforgiveness*, there was another manuscript; *"The Servant's Heart: The Road to Recovery."* At the time, I thought I was writing a book about serving well, leading with honor, and maintaining purity of heart through the different seasons of ministry. For more than twenty years I served in many capacities; behind the scenes, in leadership, and on the front lines. I had witnessed the good, the bad, the ugly and the indifferent. I wasn't writing to expose people; I was writing to reveal the process; the real journey of what it means to serve.

During the writing, something unexpected surfaced. The stories I revisited, the stretching ones, the confusing ones, the sacred ones, began touching places I thought were already healed. The pages started pulling on residue I didn't know remained. I didn't stop writing because I ran out of words; I stopped because something in the writing would not let me move forward.

I wanted *"The Servant's Heart"* to be written from a wise place, but God began to show me I was still writing from a wounded place. My pen had become a mirror, revealing not only what I lived through, but what I still carried.

There is a moment I will never forget. I was recalling a season when I was assisting my former leader. We were helping other authors with their book covers, and he loved the concepts. In conversation I said, *"I came up with the idea, and the designer brought my vision to life."* Without hesitation he said, *"That's pride."*

His words stung. Three days later, the overseer repeated the same warning at his request. The words pierced me again, and I still didn't understand because I wasn't trying to take credit. I was simply explaining the creative process. A creative process I didn't even know I had in me. Trying to write that memory exposed a place I hadn't yet examined.

I paused not because I couldn't finish the manuscript, but because God wasn't asking me to complete it. He was asking me to confront myself. So, I prayed a difficult but necessary prayer: *"Lord, if there is any pride in me, show me"*, and He did gently, clearly, layer by layer.

I began to see something I had never considered before: pride doesn't always look like arrogance. Sometimes pride looks like hurt we haven't handed over to God. Sometimes pride hides behind disappointment, silence, or the desire to be understood. Sometimes pride grows in places where language failed us and healing was delayed. That pause became my healing place. What I thought was a writing break was actually a divine reset.

It was in that stillness that this book, *"The Pride of Unforgiveness"*, was born. This time, it wasn't about what happened to me; it was about what God was uncovering in me. It wasn't about ministry roles or expectations; it was about the subtle places where pride anchors unforgiveness and hinders the heart.

This book is not about blame; it is about becoming. It is not about proving who was right; it is about choosing what is right. It is about allowing the Holy Spirit to uncover the hidden forms of pride that keep us from healing, forgiving, and serving with a whole heart again.

This is my journey written with grace, processed in truth, and completed from a healing posture and if you are reading this, perhaps the same God who confronted me is gently confronting you too. Your healing may begin with the same pause that birthed mine.

The Moment of Exposure

"Surrender your pride and power. Change your hearts before the Lord."

Jeremiah 4:4

I wasn't in prayer when it happened. I wasn't in worship or seeking revelation. I was simply getting dressed one morning, moving through my routine without expecting anything unusual. I walked into the bathroom, glanced at the mirror, and froze.

A wide shadow stretched across my chest; positioned directly over my heart. I blinked, leaned in, and tilted my body to see if it was just the lighting, but when I looked down at my actual skin, nothing was there. No bruise. No mark. No discoloration. Yet in the reflection, the shadow remained.

My first thought was natural: "What did I do in my sleep?" I'm an active sleeper, and it's not uncommon for me to wake up with bruises I can't explain, but this wasn't that. Shadows don't appear in mirrors without appearing on the body, and in my knower, I knew immediately:

The Lord was trying to show me something.

I went straight into prayer. I didn't wait to understand it on my own. As I prayed, the Holy Spirit released a phrase into my spirit, not the full verse, not the reference, just the instruction:

"Break up the fallow ground."

That's how God often speaks to me, He drops a fragment and requires me to follow Him into the Scriptures, and that morning, He led me to *Jeremiah 4.*

"Plow up the hard ground of your hearts! Do not waste your good seed among thorns. Surrender your pride and power. Change your hearts before the Lord…"

Jeremiah 4:3–4

Two parts pierced me instantly:

"Do not waste your good seed among thorns."
"Change your hearts before the Lord."

I felt those words hit the very place I didn't want to acknowledge. I had seed; good seed, pure seed, faithful seed but my heart, the ground that seed needed, had hardened in ways I hadn't noticed.

Seeing that shadow in the mirror was God confronting a truth I had not confronted within myself:

I was broken and I was convicted.

Not condemned. Convicted.

There's a difference. Conviction reveals what God is ready to heal. As I sat with that truth, the Spirit spoke again, this time not just to me:

"You are not the only one. In this season the barriers have to be removed."

That's when I realized: this shadow wasn't just my story. It was a picture of where countless others were spiritually; carrying residue, carrying wounds, carrying silent hardness that kept their hearts from receiving God's seed.

Out of that revelation, I ended up releasing this prophetic declaration at church:

"In the mighty name of Jesus, we declare that we will break up the fallow ground of our hearts, removing the barriers that have kept us from fully experiencing Your presence, Lord. We commit to sowing seeds of righteousness and truth, knowing that in due season, we shall reap a harvest of blessing if we faint not. As we plow the grounds of our hearts and yield to Your Spirit, we decree and declare a new season of spiritual awakening, renewal, and divine transformation. Let our lives be a testament to Your faithfulness and love and draw others to You in this time of revival."

That was the moment my healing began. Not when I saw the shadow, but when I surrendered to what God revealed through it.

Breaking up fallow ground is not gentle work. It is disruptive. It is uncomfortable. It is holy. But it is necessary. Pride hardens the heart. Unforgiveness dries the soil and both create ground where even the best seed cannot take root.

That morning, God exposed the shadow not to shame me, but to awaken me. It was the beginning of my breaking. The beginning of my awakening.

Introduction

Dear Reader,

There was a season when I believed forgiveness had already done its work. I prayed about it, talked about it, even testified that I had moved on. On the outside, everything looked resolved. Life continued. Ministry continued. I continued.

Yet beneath the surface, something remained unsettled. I began to question whether forgiveness had reached more than my words. It became evident that functioning and freedom were not the same thing. Pride had quietly convinced me that because I could keep going, I must be healed. But the heart remembers what language avoids.

There were still places carrying residue I had not yet confronted. I found myself reacting to moments that no longer existed, rehearsing emotions tied to experiences I claimed I had released. What I called strength was often survival, and what I labeled peace was sometimes avoidance. That tension marked the beginning of a deeper work—one that required more than confession. It required surrender.

If you are holding this book, I believe God is inviting you into that same deeper honesty. Maybe you've said the words, *"I forgive you,"* yet something still tightens in your chest when their name surfaces. You smile, you serve, you show up. Yet your soul still remembers. That is not weakness. It is a sign that God desires to heal you more deeply than you have allowed yourself to be healed.

Forgiveness is not a one-time moment. It is a continual agreement to let God touch what pride tries to protect. It is choosing truth over the illusion of *"I'm fine."* Many of us don't realize we're still bound because we've learned how to dress our pain in strength and call it maturity. We've learned how to cope, not how to be free.

This book is your invitation to pause and be honest, not with the world, but with God and with yourself. Together, we will uncover the ways pride hides behind self-protection, how unresolved offense disguises itself as discernment, and how partial forgiveness quietly drains your peace. But more than that, we'll walk into the kind of release that restores your clarity, your voice, and your capacity to love again.

You are not wrong for still feeling what you feel. You are not behind. You are not broken beyond repair. You are simply being called into a deeper kind of release; one you can live, not just speak.

As you turn these pages, allow each **Heart Pause**, every **Heart Posture Check**, and each **Prophetic Nudge** to gently slow you and draw you closer to the heart of God. At the end of each chapter, you'll be invited into an **Integration Moment**—a brief space to sit with what has surfaced, reflect without pressure, and allow truth to settle beyond the page. This is the place where forgiveness deepens, pride loosens its grip, and rest begins to take root. Let this journey become your altar of honesty and a pathway toward lasting freedom.

This is not just another book about forgiveness. It is a realignment — a heart reset, and a call to maturity and wholeness. You don't have to pretend you're over it; you can actually begin to walk in freedom.

Let's walk this out together.

With grace and truth,
Temeila Daniel

CHAPTER 1
The Silent Bondage of Unforgiveness

Governing Scripture: *Matthew 6:14 (NLT)*

"If you forgive those who sin against you, your heavenly Father will forgive you."

Prophetic Nudge

Freedom does not begin when they apologize. Freedom begins the moment you say, *"Lord, I release them."* Heaven responds to your surrender long before people respond to your pain.

The Weight You Learn to Carry

There was a season when I believed forgiveness had already been addressed. I said the words out loud, wrote names on pieces of paper, and laid them on the altar. Then, in one of the hardest but most freeing acts of obedience, I burned the letters. Watching the flames rise felt symbolic, as if the weight I carried was turning into ash before my eyes. Even as the smoke lifted, one thing became clear: the burning was symbolic, but the believing would still be tested.

Like the prophet Elisha who burned his plow and oxen before following Elijah *(1 Kings 19:21)*, I intended to close the door to an old season so I could step fully into the new. But in time, it became evident that while the fire consumed the paper, it had not yet touched everything in my heart.

Symbolic acts have power, but they do not replace surrender.

Unforgiveness doesn't always scream through anger or bitterness. Sometimes it whispers through silence. It hides behind busy schedules, ministry assignments, and emotional numbness. You learn to function, to lead, to show up, but the wound still speaks when pressed. Unforgiveness is an invisible weight. It won't stop you from walking, but it can and will make every step heavier.

Heart Pause

Take a breath.

Not to reopen what hurt you, but to acknowledge that God is here and you are safe.

You don't have to defend your pain.

You don't have to pretend you're beyond it.

Let this pause loosen the grip unforgiveness has held on your heart. Freedom begins with honesty, not pressure.

The Trap of Pride

At the root of that silent weight, pride was present. Pride told me I had moved on. Pride told me revisiting the pain would make me look weak. Pride told me I was justified in keeping my distance. Pride even tried to convince me that forgiveness meant letting someone off the hook.

Listen, deep beneath all that self-protection was a harder truth: My heart wanted justice more than it wanted peace.

That is how pride disguises itself. It convinces you that holding on is strength. It whispers, *"They need to feel what they did to you."* I need you to know that pride is never invested in healing… it's invested in control, and while pride guards the wound, grace stands outside the gate waiting to be invited back in.

The Spiritual Law of Release

Jesus never separated forgiveness from freedom. He made it clear: *"If you forgive… your Father will forgive you." **(Matthew 6:14)*** Forgiveness isn't about fairness, it's about flow. When forgiveness is withheld, spiritual blockages begin to form:

- Prayer becomes strained.
- Peace becomes short-lived.
- Joy requires effort.
- Vision loses clarity.

Forgiveness restores the flow where bitterness once slowed it.

Healing Hidden Offense

Some offenses are loud; betrayal, lies, abandonment. Others are quiet, unmet expectations, subtle disappointments, unspoken wounds. Both create residue when left unaddressed.

You may not talk about it anymore, but if you still rehearse it internally, it still owns space spiritually.

Psalm 34:18 reminds us: *"The Lord is close to the brokenhearted; He rescues those whose spirits are crushed."*

True healing begins the moment you let God touch what pride has tried to hide.

Heart Work, Not Lip Service

Forgiveness is not a sentence we speak; it is soil we tend until no roots of bitterness remain. You'll know release has taken root when:

- The memory no longer stings.
- You can bless them sincerely.
- You no longer need closure to feel peace.

It is possible to say ***"I forgive you"*** while your heart says something else entirely. That's why God doesn't look for language, He looks for surrender.

I have always desired to keep my heart pure before God. I never wanted to be the kind of minister who teaches powerfully but bleeds privately. Someone who can communicate truth with clarity yet still carry unhealed wounds beneath the surface. My desire has always been to serve from wholeness, not from hurt and to pour out love not filtered through pain. As I continued serving, it became increasingly clear that unaddressed residue has a way of affecting even the most sincere work.

Heart Posture Check

- o Whose name still tightens something in me?
- o Have I confused avoidance with peace?
- o What part of me still needs to be right?

Prayer

Father, expose every place where unforgiveness still lives in me. Lift the residue I have carried in silence.

Break the power of pride and give me courage to surrender what **my** strength tried to protect. Touch the places I have avoided and heal the wounds I learned to function around. Today, I choose release. Today, I choose peace. Today, I choose forgiveness. In Jesus' name, Amen.

Integration Moment 1: Release

Governing Scripture: *Psalm 51:10*

"Create in me a clean heart, O God. Renew a loyal spirit within me."

God never intended for you to carry what He has already conquered. Today, let release be your first act of obedience — not to feel free yet, but to make room for freedom to begin.

Heart Pause

What have you been holding that God has already asked you to release?

Prayer

God, I pause here without explanation. I don't try to fix what surfaced. I don't rush past what You revealed. I lay down what I've been holding — even the things I don't yet have words for. Sit with me in this space. I give You my consent to work beneath my understanding. I yield what feels unfinished.

I release what feels heavy. I trust You with what I cannot yet articulate. In Jesus' name, Amen.

CHAPTER 2
Pride: The Root Beneath the Bitterness

Governing Scripture: *Proverbs 16:18 (KJV)*

"Pride goeth before destruction, and an haughty spirit before a fall."

Prophetic Nudge

Pride often hides beneath pain, but surrender exposes it. Ask the Lord to show you where self-protection has replaced trust and willingly lay that place before Him.

The Subtle Root

Bitterness never begins as bitterness; it begins as pride dressed in pain. It whispers, *"I didn't deserve this."* That part is valid. Now, I need you to understand this, if the heart sits with that truth too long, it shifts. Pride steps in quietly, convincing you that protection is safety and that distance is discernment. What feels like strength becomes a shield — not of faith, but of self-preservation.

Unforgiveness is often assumed to be only emotional residue, but pride operates as its hidden root system. We see the fruit — resentment, isolation, defensiveness — but beneath the surface is pride, feeding the offense and choking out grace. You can pull at the fruit forever, but until the root is exposed, nothing truly changes.

When Pride Hides as Strength

Pride doesn't always roar; sometimes it looks like composure.

It says,

"I'm fine," when your soul is weary.

It says,

"I don't need to talk about it," when confession would heal.

It says,

"I've moved on," when the heart is still anchored to the wound.

Silence is often mistaken for maturity. I thought strength meant not showing emotion; not letting anyone see the tears, the questions, or the ache. But maturity without humility is hardness in disguise.

True strength is not the absence of pain; it is the presence of surrender. Until your heart comes out from behind the armor, God cannot touch what pride is protecting.

Heart Pause

Breathe for a moment.

Let your shoulders drop.

You do not have to defend your pain here.

You do not have to pretend you're over it.

This is where God begins to untangle what you have learned to normalize. Let Him soften the places where pride hardened you for survival.

Pride's Three Masks

Pride rarely announces itself; it disguises itself as wisdom, caution, or strength. But beneath every disguise is the same agenda: self-preservation. Pride convinces you that protecting yourself is the same as healing yourself. It persuades you that control is safety, that distance is peace, and that silence is strength.

Here are the faces pride often wears:

1. Self-Righteousness

Convincing yourself you handled things better than the other person. It keeps you rehearsing the narrative where you are the one who "rose above."

2. Self-Protection

Building walls so high that even God has to knock to get in. It feels like boundaries, but it is actually emotional barricading.

3. Self-Reliance

Trying to heal yourself without letting the Holy Spirit reach the deeper places. It looks like independence, but it becomes isolation.

Each mask blocks honesty.

Pride isolates; humility invites.

Pride explains; humility surrenders.

Pride covers; humility exposes to heal.

A Moment of Clarity

One morning in prayer, the Lord spoke so clearly:

"You cannot properly serve Me until you get free."

Those words brought immediate clarity — not as condemnation, but as clarity. I had been trying to serve God while still carrying the weight of old wounds, believing I could push through pain and still pour out purity. But Heaven was not after performance — Heaven was after freedom.

My ability to lead, love, discern, and even hear God clearly was connected to my willingness to release. Pride convinced me that I was functioning. God reminded me that He wanted me free.

I broke that morning. Not because I was ashamed, but because I was being cleansed. I realized that deliverance was not only for others, but it was also for me as well. From that day forward,

I made a vow: **I would not minister from memory. I would minister from healing.**

What is Ministering from Memory?

Ministering from memory is serving from unresolved experiences rather than from healed ones. It occurs when a person continues to lead, give, or pour out while certain places of the heart have learned how to function without being restored. The work continues, but the wound remains unaddressed.

How It Appears

Ministering from memory does not always interrupt service, but it does affect how a person carries it.

It often shows up as:

- Guarded engagement in familiar situations

- Emotional distance paired with continued commitment

- Defensiveness framed as discernment

- Strength drawn from survival rather than freedom

The individual is not being dishonest. They are functioning from patterns that once protected them but were never meant to lead them.

Why Memory Cannot Govern

When memory leads:

- Past experiences interpret present interactions

- Old disappointments influence current responses

    Protection replaces trust

- Effort replaces rest

Over time, this creates internal strain. What once helped sustain a season begins to limit clarity, peace, and capacity.

The Difference Between Remembering and Being Healed

Healing does not erase memory.
It removes its authority.

A healed heart may remember what occurred, but it no longer reacts from it. The experience loses its power to shape decisions, posture, and response.

Memory reacts based on familiarity.
Healing responds from truth.

Why This Matters

God addresses ministering from memory because longevity in service requires internal freedom.

"So Christ has truly set us free. Now make sure that you stay free, and don't get tied up again in slavery to the law."

Galatians 5:1

Survival may sustain a person for a time, but it cannot carry them forward without cost. What was once necessary for endurance must eventually give way to restoration.

This is not about disqualification.

It is about alignment.

Heart Posture Check

- o Do I defend my pain more than I surrender it?
- o Have I confused being guarded with being wise?
- o Where am I rehearsing the story instead of releasing it?

Prayer

Father, I acknowledge the places where pride has lived in my heart. I confess where self-protection replaced trust and where silence felt safer than surrender. I lay down the need to guard what You are ready to heal. Teach me humility where fear once led and truth where pride once justified. In Jesus' name, Amen.

Integration Moment 2: Renewal

Governing Scripture: *Romans 12:2*

"Don't copy the behavior and customs of this world, but let God transform you into a new person by changing the way you think. Then you will learn to know God's will for you, which is good and pleasing and perfect."

Renewal begins in the mind. Notice what you've been replaying and intentionally place those thoughts before God. A renewed mind does not deny pain — it refuses to let pain define truth.

Heart Pause

What thought has tried to become truth in your mind that God is calling you to surrender?

Prayer

Lord, renew my thoughts until they agree with Heaven. Teach my thoughts to agree with truth over self-protection. Align my mind with peace and anchor me in Your truth. In Jesus' name, Amen.

CHAPTER 3
When "I Deserve Better" Becomes an Idol

Governing Scripture: *Romans 12:3*

"Because of the privilege and authority God has given me, I give each of you this warning: Don't think you are better than you really are. Be honest in your evaluation of yourselves, measuring yourselves by the faith God has given us."

Prophetic Nudge

Entitlement disguises itself as empowerment, but it quietly repositions the heart. It dethrones God one expectation at a time. The Lord is calling you back to a place where gratitude outweighs grievance and surrender becomes sweeter than self-defense.

The Subtle Shift

There is a moment when honest pain begins to echo something different. A moment when *"I didn't deserve that"* quietly transforms into *"I deserve better."*

One is truth.

The other becomes a posture.

If the heart lingers too long in the first statement, it naturally drifts into the second. What started as acknowledging hurt subtly reshapes into entitlement.

The shift is quiet, almost unnoticeable:

"I deserved better treatment."

"I deserved better support."

"I deserved a better outcome."

"I deserved something different from God."

Grief transforms into demand.

Disappointment becomes doctrine.

Expectation becomes entitlement.

That is the moment pride begins rewriting the narrative.

The Idol of Entitlement

Pride does not begin with arrogance; it begins with unexamined expectation.

Expectation is human.

Entitlement is expectation turned into a claim.

Here's how entitlement speaks:

"Because I obeyed, God owes me this outcome."

"Because I served, He owes me this blessing."

"Because I endured, He owes me restoration in the form I imagined."

Entitlement builds altars in places God never required worship. It binds the heart to an outcome, not to obedience. It makes you worship what should happen instead of the God who holds all things together.

Jesus dismantled entitlement in one sentence:

"When you obey Me, say: 'We are unworthy servants who have simply done our duty.'" **Luke 17:10**

Grace is not earned.

Breakthrough is not a paycheck.

Blessing is not compensation.

God is not obligated.

Entitlement feeds on expectation. Humility feeds on gratitude.

Heart Pause

Breathe deeply.

Allow space for reflection where a true *"I didn't deserve that"* quietly shifted into *"I deserve better."* There is no shame here — only clarity. God never reveals to condemn; He reveals to free.

A Moment of Reckoning

I remember one evening when I mentally listed everything I had poured out —every yes, every sacrifice, every assignment completed without complaint. Outwardly I was calm, but inwardly my heart was pouting. My spirit was rehearsing a quiet accusation: *"God, You owe me something for all of this."*

In that moment, the Father — gentle, patient, unbothered by my internal frustration, impressed this truth upon my heart:

"Learn to see Me in the small things."

At first, I was like, *"Whaaat?"* Then that sentence unraveled me. It softened what had hardened around my heart. He reminded me that He had been present all along:

He was there in the peace that met me every morning.

He was there in the strength that carried me through assignments.

He was there in the song in my spirit each day.

He was there in the unexpected encouragements, the quiet victories, the daily bread.

That night, I repented.

I repented not because I was ashamed, but because entitlement had blinded me to God's daily goodness. It became evident that I had been measuring God by moments instead of by His nature.

It wasn't that He wasn't blessing me, it's that I had stopped recognizing it. Gratitude restored what entitlement tried to distort. Humility reopened what pride tried to shut.

When Comparison Fuels Entitlement Entitlement rarely travels alone; comparison often walks beside it. We look at someone else's breakthrough and quietly wonder:

"Why them first?"

"What about me?"

"God, haven't I waited long enough?"

Comparison converts gratitude into grievance and perception into pressure.

When Peter compared his journey to John's, Jesus redirected him with these words:

"If I want him to remain until I return, what is that to you? As for you, follow Me." **John 21:22**

The cure for comparison is focus.

The cure for entitlement is surrender.

Both return you to your rightful posture.

Heart Posture Check

- Have I turned obedience into negotiation with God?
- Do I serve expecting a specific outcome?
- Where have I compared my timeline to someone else's?

Prayer

Father, forgive me for the places where expectation turned into entitlement. I repent for measuring Your goodness by outcomes and allowing disappointment to speak louder than trust. Restore gratitude where demand has lived and humility where comparison has crept in. I release the need to be owed and return my heart to obedience and trust. In Jesus' name, Amen.

Integration Moment 3: Realignment

Governing Scripture: *Proverbs 3:5–6*

"Trust in the Lord with all your heart; do not depend on your own understanding. Seek his will in all you do, and he will show you which path to take."

Realignment is not punishment — it is protection. When your heart drifts, pause and return to trust. Realignment begins when you release the need to understand and choose to follow God's lead again. He is not forcing a detour — He is restoring your direction.

Heart Pause

Where has your heart drifted, and what is God inviting you to bring back into alignment?

Prayer

Holy Spirit, draw my desires into agreement with Your design. Reposition my steps. Restore my sensitivity. Bring me back into the center of Your will. In Jesus' name, Amen.

CHAPTER 4
The Illusion of Forgiveness

Governing Scripture: *Matthew 15:8*

"These people honor Me with their lips, but their hearts are far from Me."

Prophetic Nudge

There are moments when we believe forgiveness has taken root, but Heaven knows the difference between spoken release and surrendered release. Sometimes our words sound healed, while our hearts are still holding memory. This is an invitation to pause — not to analyze yourself, but to let God show you what may still be hidden beneath your confession.

Lip Service vs. Heart Surrender

There was a season when I was convinced I had fully forgiven. I prayed the prayers, said the right words, and even testified about release as if it had already taken place. I genuinely believed time had healed what truth had not yet touched.

I know this truth may sound familiar. That is intentional. God often returns us to the same place until we are able to hear what we have avoided without flinching. What felt like repetition was really Heaven pressing the same truth deeper without flinching. Each moment felt like a new revelation, but it was really Heaven saying the same thing again:

"You've said you've forgiven, but your heart still remembers differently."

That realization arrested me. How could I love God, serve people, and still carry residue in places no one could see? But that is how illusion works.

Forgiveness is not proven by vocabulary. It is revealed by posture. You can speak release and still protect resentment. You can lift your hands in worship while your heart quietly holds the reins of justice. I was close to God with my lips, yet my heart was still guarding old wounds as if they needed my protection.

The Signs of Surface Forgiveness

As this became clearer, the signs of surface forgiveness began to emerge; the kind that appears spiritual but avoids surrender.

It shows up as:

- Avoiding the person instead of addressing the pain.
- Referencing the situation only to highlight personal growth.
- Blessing publicly while blaming privately.
- Releasing the event but retaining the emotion.

These are not signs of deliverance. They are signs of delay. Until your emotions agree with your confession, forgiveness remains incomplete. Peace is postponed, not possessed.

Heart Pause

Take a breath here.

Not to defend yourself — but to allow truth to settle.

This is not about shame. It is about clarity.

God exposes residue because He loves us too much to let fragments of offense take root in places He is trying to rebuild with grace.

When Forgiveness Becomes Performance

There was a time I believed saying, "I'm over it," meant I was mature. But performance is not healing. It is self-protection wrapped in spiritual language.

You cannot fake peace.

You can only delay confrontation.

God, being who He is, will always return us to the place of offense — not to reopen the wound, but to remove the infection.

For a long while, I felt guilty for still feeling anything at all. I assumed real forgiveness meant never thinking about it again, but healing often comes in layers. Some wounds require more than one *"yes"* before they are fully released.

One morning, a clear truth settled in my spirit:

"I don't need you to be numb. I need you to be honest."

That sentence changed everything.

God was never asking me to pretend it didn't happen. He was asking me to let Him touch the places I kept trying to harden. Each time I brought the person, the memory, or the conversation back before Him, something lifted. Not always instantly, but always intentionally.

Forgiveness is not weakness.

Forgiveness is warfare.

It is choosing grace repeatedly until peace becomes your posture.

Heart Posture Check

- o   Do I forgive to move on, or to move closer to God?
- o   Have I confused avoidance with peace?
- o   Have I forgiven with my words but withheld my emotions from God?

Prayer

Father, I bring You what I've tried to cover with words. I admit where I've said I forgave, but still felt the weight of the memory. I stop performing peace and allow You into what still feels tender. I give You permission to heal what I've only managed. Make forgiveness real in me — not just spoken but settled. In Jesus' name, Amen.

Integration Moment 4: Honest Surrender

Governing Scripture: *Psalm 139:23-24*

"Search me, O God, and know my heart; test me and know my anxious thoughts. Point out anything in me that offends You, and lead me along the path of everlasting life."

Forgiveness does not deepen through denial — it deepens through honesty. This moment is not about fixing what surfaced; it is about allowing God to touch what your words may have covered. You are not regressing because something still feels tender. You are responding to truth. Stay present here, without explaining or defending. Healing continues where honesty is welcomed.

Heart Pause

What emotion have you released with your words but not yet surrendered to God?

Prayer

Father, I give You permission to search my heart without resistance. I bring You what still feels unresolved, unguarded by performance or language.

Teach me how to forgive with my whole heart, not just my confession. I trust You with what is still tender. In Jesus' name, Amen.

CHAPTER 5
The Cycle of Control

Governing Scripture: *James 4:6–7*

"And he gives grace generously. As the Scriptures say, 'God opposes the proud but gives grace to the humble.' So humble yourselves before God. Resist the devil, and he will flee from you."

Prophetic Nudge

Control doesn't enter loudly; it slips in quietly where trust has been wounded. It shapes how you think, how you respond, and how you protect yourself. God never exposes control to shame you; He exposes it to set you free. This is your invitation to unclench your fist, breathe again, and let Him reclaim the places where fear pretended to be strength.

When Forgiveness Doesn't Feel Safe

There's a truth many never say out loud: sometimes forgiveness feels dangerous. After betrayal, humiliation, or mishandled trust, the heart begins building fences — not because you're bitter, but because you're trying to survive. At first those fences look like healthy boundaries. Without healing, fences evolve into fortresses and fortresses don't just keep danger out — they keep God out too.

During a time of deep wounding, I told myself I was *"Protecting my Peace."* But a sobering truth began to surface: I wasn't protecting peace. I was protecting control. Pain had discipled me into tightening my grip when healing actually required me to release it.

I started managing outcomes, rehearsing conversations, even anticipating disappointments, not because I wanted power, but because I feared pain. Here's the deception: Control feels like safety, but in the spirit, it is suffocation. Control is the counterfeit comfort of the wounded.

The Hidden Pattern:

Pain → Pride → Control → Isolation

Pain enters through offense, rejection, or disappointment. Pride steps in and whispers, *"You won't hurt me again."* Control becomes the armor. Isolation becomes the lifestyle and because it's quiet, you'll call the isolation *"peace,"* when it's really distance dressed as deliverance. Pride doesn't always strut, sometimes it hides behind independence. Independence is not healing. Independence is the refusal to be touched in the places that still ache. Healing flows through connection, not control. Whenever we try to fix what only God can heal, our miracle gets delayed.

Heart Pause

Breathe.

Not to revisit the pain, but to acknowledge the pattern. God is not exposing control to embarrass you; He is showing you where your heart got tired of trusting. What feels like exposure is really invitation. This is where the cycle begins to break.

The Illusion of Safety

There was a season where I convinced myself that holding everything together made me dependable, mature, and strong. One day, in prayer, this truth settled in my spirit:

"You're not holding it together — you're holding Me out. Let Me in."

Those words unraveled me. I began to see that I had built walls even He wasn't invited to climb. My control wasn't protecting me; it was blocking His presence.

What you refuse to release will eventually rule you.

The very thing you think you've mastered becomes the quiet master over your peace.

A Personal Surrender: Letting God Be God Again

There came a day when I was trying to "fix" a situation I didn't create, yet I felt responsible to repair. I prayed, strategized, even rehearsed what I'd say; as if the right approach could force reconciliation. The Lord whispered again: *"That's My assignment, not yours."* I sat with that.

Letting go didn't mean defeat. It meant deliverance. It meant allowing God to do what my control could never accomplish. When I surrendered the outcome, peace returned. My prayer shifted from*: "Lord, fix it,"* to *"Lord, free me.",* and He did.

Heart Posture Check

- o Where am I trying to fix what only God can heal?
- o Have I mistaken stewardship for control?
- o What part of my heart still believes, "If I don't handle it, it won't get done"?

Let God speak here. This is where chains loosen.

Prayer

Father, forgive me for the places I've carried control like armor. Teach me to trust Your timing, Your wisdom, and Your way. Loosen my grip where fear has tightened it. Reveal the difference between stewardship and striving. I release every outcome, every person, and every situation I have tried to manage. Let humility open what pride once closed. Let peace return where fear has been ruling. In Jesus' name, Amen.

Integration Moment 5: REFILL

Governing Scripture: *John 7:38*

"Anyone who believes in me may come and drink! For the Scriptures declare, 'Rivers of living water will flow from his heart.'"

You cannot pour from what is empty — and God never asked you to. Refill begins where control ends. When you release the need to manage outcomes, you make room for God to replenish what striving has drained. This moment is not about doing more, but about receiving again from the true source.

Heart Pause

Where have you been running on empty, and what part of you is God trying to refill today?

Prayer

Lord, refill me until overflow becomes natural. Breathe life into dry wells and awaken fresh rivers within me. Restore every place where striving has stolen strength and teach me to receive from You as my source and supply. In Jesus' name, Amen.

CHAPTER 6
When God Rewrites the Story

Governing Scripture: *Romans 8:28*

"And we know that God causes everything to work together for the good of those who love God and are called according to His purpose for them."

Prophetic Nudge

God never asks you to hand Him the pen without intention. When He rewrites a chapter of your life, He is not erasing your reality — He is redeeming its meaning. Release your interpretation of what happened and intentionally return that chapter to Him. What once wounded can now instruct. What once broke you can now build you. Grace is not editing your past — it is reframing your future.

The Pain That Tried to Define You

Pain is persuasive. It tries to stamp your identity with its own language:

Rejected.

Overlooked.

Betrayed.

Used.

Forgotten.

If you're not watchful, you begin living as if one painful moment is the whole story.

I had times where disappointment became louder than destiny. Trauma tried to become truth. I began interpreting myself through what I survived rather than what God had spoken. But here is the truth that reframes everything: Pain is not your author — God is. He is the author and finisher of our faith. When we rehearse what hurt us, we give pain the pen. When we surrender that chapter back to God, we return authorship to the One who always writes in purpose.

I once prayed through a situation I could not mentally release, and the Lord whispered:

"I am reclaiming the time. Let Me rewrite it."

He wasn't ignoring what happened. He was overturning its interpretation.

Divine Editing — Letting God Take the Pen

The Holy Spirit is the divine editor of the healed heart.

He doesn't delete your story. He redeems your sight. He doesn't erase the memory. He removes the sting. He doesn't alter the event. He alters its authority.

The very moment meant to weaken you becomes the moment God uses to strengthen someone else. The page you wanted to rip out becomes the page your deliverance stands on.

One day I reread an old journal entry that once brought tears of devastation, and I realized I could read it without breaking. That is what divine editing looks like. Not the absence of memory, but the absence of torment.

Heart Pause

Let your spirit breathe.

God is not rewriting your story to make it prettier. He's rewriting it to make you clearer.

The Process of Revision

Every story goes through drafts. The first draft of your life was written in real time — unfiltered and raw, but restoration is the revision process. As God heals you, He lifts the weight off old pages. He rewrites your understanding. He reveals the wisdom beneath the wound. Some pages stay the same, but you don't. That's the miracle.

When you let God revise your story: Pain loses its authority. Shame loses its voice. Memory loses its ability to define you. Purpose becomes louder than the past. You stop living in the version written by pain and begin living in the version authored by grace.

A Personal Reflection — Becoming Through the Breaking

When I look back now at the moments that nearly crushed me, I see how they carved compassion into me. What once produced bitterness now births boldness. What once silenced me now gives me vocabulary for others. Your story becomes a tool in the hands of a faithful God.

Nothing wasted.

Nothing random.

Nothing without redemption.

Heart Posture Check

- o What am I still allowing to define me that God has already redeemed?
- o Where is God trying to revise my understanding?
- o Am I willing to surrender the narrative I've held onto for the one He is writing?

Prayer

Father, thank You for being the Author and Finisher of my faith. Rewrite what pain attempted to define and restore the pages where sorrow lingered. Redeem the parts of my story I still struggle to understand and remove the authority of what no longer aligns with Your truth. I surrender the pen to You — write Your purpose fully in me. In Jesus' name, Amen.

Integration Moment 6: Reposition

Governing Scripture: *Isaiah 43:19*

"For I am about to do something new. See, I have already begun! Do you not see it? I will make a pathway through the wilderness. I will create rivers in the dry wasteland."

Repositioning is not punishment — it is perspective. When God shifts your understanding, He is not removing you from your destiny; He is restoring authorship over it. What once defined you no longer has authority to narrate your future. This moment invites you to release old interpretations and allow God to reframe what happened through His truth.

Repositioning begins internally, when you agree to see the past through redemption instead of pain.

Heart Pause

What meaning have you attached to this experience that God is asking you to release so He can reframe it?

Prayer

Father, reposition my understanding and realign my perspective with Your truth. Remove interpretations that no longer serve healing, and restore clarity where pain once spoke loudest. I surrender my view and trust You to reveal Your meaning. In Jesus' name, Amen.

CHAPTER 7
Learning the Unforced Rhythms of Grace

Governing Scripture: *Matthew 11:28–30 (MSG)*

"Are you tired? Worn out? Burned out on religion? Come to me. Get away with me and you'll recover your life. I'll show you how to take a real rest. Walk with me and work with me—watch how I do it. Learn the unforced rhythms of grace. I won't lay anything heavy or ill-fitting on you. Keep company with me and you'll learn to live freely and lightly."

Prophetic Nudge

Grace carries a rhythm, and heaven carries a pace. When your steps align with God's cadence, pressure breaks, striving melts, and rest becomes revelation. This is your invitation to release every pace that never came from Him and return to the sound of His peace.

Spiritual Arrhythmia — When the Soul Loses Its Beat

In medicine, arrhythmia occurs when the heart's rhythm becomes irregular—too fast, too slow, or completely off-beat. When the rhythm is off, strength fades, dizziness follows, and the body struggles to circulate life. The same thing happens to the soul when it drifts out of rhythm with God. We begin pushing beyond grace, performing without peace, and living spiritually dizzy—busy but out of breath. It's not unbelief; it's misalignment. We start beating to the wrong tempo.

When pride, pain, or pressure override presence, we develop spiritual arrhythmia. We move faster than grace was designed to carry us. We confuse momentum with movement and wonder why our hearts feel faint.

But Jesus whispers: ***"Walk with Me, and watch how I do it."***

The cure isn't speed — it's alignment. Healing begins when your heartbeat syncs with heaven again.

Heart Pause

Take a moment and breathe.

Let your spirit settle.

Grace doesn't demand speed — it invites alignment. Let God restore the rhythm you were created to carry.

When Stillness Becomes Sound

Grace doesn't rush — it flows. It's a divine tempo set by peace, not pressure. Stillness isn't silence; it's a new sound. When your spirit slows enough to listen, heaven's cadence becomes clear. His voice grows familiar. And the beat of your life begins to sync with His again.

There is a sacredness in quiet obedience — the kind that doesn't need to prove movement but stays submitted to His pace. Sometimes God isn't asking you to go farther or faster — He's calling you to listen deeper. When you live in step with grace, you stop competing with someone else's pace and start completing your own purpose.

Grace doesn't hurry you; it heals you. It doesn't pressure you; it positions you.

Heart Posture Check

- o Where have I been out of rhythm with grace?
- o Have I been performing for God instead of partnering with Him?
- o What does walking — not running — with God look like for me right now?

Prayer

Father, tune my heart to Your rhythm again. Where I've been restless, bring rest. Where I've been rushing, teach me to walk with You. Align my pace with Your grace. Let my soul find peace in Your timing and strength in Your stillness. Restore harmony where life has felt offbeat and let my days move in the unforced rhythm of Your love. In Jesus' name, Amen.

Integration Moment 7: Resettling

Governing Scripture: *John 21:17*

"He said to him the third time, 'Simon son of John, do you love me?' Peter was hurt that Jesus asked the question a third time. He said, 'Lord, you know everything. You know that I love you.' Jesus said, 'Then feed my sheep.'"

Rest does not remove purpose — it restores it. Before function resumes, rhythm must be reset. This moment is not about what you are called to do next, but about learning how to remain with God without striving. Let love, not pressure, become the measure again.

Heart Pause

Where might God be inviting you to remain with Him rather than rush back into function?

Prayer

Lord, teach me how to stay with You without proving anything. Restore my rhythm, not my pressure. Let love lead my pace and rest guard my purpose. I choose alignment over urgency. In Jesus' name, Amen.

CHAPTER 8
The Spirit That Twists

Governing Scripture: *Job 41:34 (KJV)*

"He beholdeth all high things: he is a king over all the children of pride."

Prophetic Nudge

There are moments when clarity feels close, yet communication feels strained. That tension is never random. When truth is challenged, the enemy often targets perception. Pause before responding, choose humility over assumption, and let grace untangle what pride tries to twist.

The Hidden War Beneath Words

There are battles that begin long before action — battles that start in perception. It's the war that erupts when a word is misunderstood, a tone is misread, or a motive is assumed. This is the territory Scripture associates with Leviathan — a twisting spirit that distorts communication and feeds pride through misunderstanding.

Call It What It Is — The Spirit of Leviathan

Throughout Scripture, Leviathan is described as both serpent and sea creature — a twisting spirit that operates in deep waters.

Isaiah 27:1 calls him "the piercing serpent, the crooked serpent… the dragon that is in the sea." In *Job 41*, he is described as untamable, fierce, and proud — "king over all the children of pride."

- Like a serpent, he twists truth subtly.
- Like a sea creature, he stirs waves of confusion and offense.

His mission is consistent — to distort, divide, and disrupt unity. Where pride refuses correction, Leviathan thrives. Where offense festers, he coils tighter. But where humility reigns, he loses his grip.

Heart Pause

Take a breath.

Discernment sharpens when the heart grows quiet. God reveals what the enemy twists so truth can rise above assumption.

The Twisting of Truth

Leviathan's greatest weapon is distortion. He bends what was said until it no longer resembles the original intent. He makes you hear through pain, speak through pride, and respond through fear.

Before long, clarity becomes confusion, connection becomes conflict, and partnership becomes suspicion. This is why communication is sacred in the Kingdom. Words build relational bridges, and Leviathan seeks to break them. If he can twist perception, he can sabotage purpose.

I've seen it in ministry, families, and friendships — where one conversation misheard through the ears of pride unraveled years of trust. A misunderstanding became separation because no one paused to humble themselves and clarify.

The Cure: Humility and Stillness

Leviathan suffocates where humility and stillness dwell. He survives on reaction, accusation, defensiveness, and the need to be right. But when you ask, *"Lord, show me what's true,"* his coils begin to loosen.

God once told me, "Don't respond to the twist, speak to the truth." That became my anchor whenever confusion tried to enter conversations or assignments. I learned that peace is preserved not by winning arguments but by maintaining alignment.

James 4:6 (KJV) reminds, *"God resisteth the proud, but giveth grace unto the humble."*

Humility is Heaven's resistance system. It disarms the twisting spirit and restores clear vision.

Heart Posture Check

- o Do I listen to understand or to defend?
- o Have I allowed offense to become my interpreter?
- o Where have I reacted instead of responding in grace?

Prayer

Father, reveal every area where truth has been twisted in my perception. Expose pride that has hidden behind misunderstanding and give me grace to respond with humility instead of defense. Restore clarity where confusion has lived and peace where offense once spoke loudest. Let Your truth govern how I hear, speak, and respond. In Jesus' name, Amen.

Integration Moment 8: Recalibrate

Governing Scripture: *Proverbs 4:23*
"Guard your heart above all else, for it determines the course of your life."

When distortion has been exposed, you cannot keep moving the same way. This is the moment your spirit recalibrates. Recalibration is Heaven adjusting your internal settings — how you hear, how you see, how you interpret, how you speak, how you respond, and how you guard your heart.

Leviathan twists.

Recalibration untangles.

Leviathan confuses.

Recalibration clarifies.

Leviathan fuels pride.

Recalibration anchors humility.

This reset is not about fighting — it is about fine-tuning. It is God restoring clarity to your perception so you can hear differently, see differently, and respond from truth instead of triggers.

Heart Pause

Where might God be adjusting how you perceive, interpret, or respond so your heart remains guarded in truth?

Prayer

Father, recalibrate my heart, my hearing, and my discernment. Adjust every place where distortion tried to lead. Restore truth to my perception and humility to my posture. Untangle what pride complicated and reset what pain misaligned. Lead me in clarity, purity, and truth. In Jesus' name, Amen.

PART II
The Prayer Room

THE PRAYER ROOM
The Interior Life of a Restored Heart

Before you step into rest, you must step into stillness.

Before you step into peace, you must reconnect to Presence.

The Prayer Room is not a place — it is a posture. It is where your heart breathes again. Everyone who journeys through healing must enter this room, because healing is incomplete without communion, and restoration is incomplete without connection.

The Prayer Room becomes the space where emotions quiet, the spirit centers, the heart listens, the soul softens, posture aligns, and discernment deepens.

This isn't reserved for intercessors. This is for anyone who has walked through the pages of this book with me on my healing journey. This is where I truly found my Prayer Room. I had never prayed this much in my whole entire life.

After all was said and done, I was able to sit with God again but differently. You may find that you need to sit with Him again in a different posture.

It is in this room where my healing was sealed, rest was restored, and identity was rebuilt and I am truly thankful.

The Posture of the Restored Heart

Before you speak, you must see.

Before you ask, you must listen.

Before you pour out, you must pause.

A restored heart does not pray from panic — it prays from presence. It does not intercede from exhaustion — it intercedes from alignment.

It does not watch from fear — it watches from rest.

True prayer is not performance. It is the quiet turning of the heart toward God until your heartbeat and His begin to move in the same rhythm.

Four Prayer Focuses of the Restored Heart

1. For Your Own Heart

Father, steady my emotions, settle my thoughts, and let my heart find its rest in You. Heal where I'm tender. Strengthen where I'm empty. Speak where I'm listening.

2. For Those Connected to Your Life

Lord, fortify the hearts of those I love. Cover their minds, anchor their steps, and align them with Your peace. Let unity and understanding flow.

3. For the Church

Awaken unity. Uproot pride. Restore humility and purity. Make us a people who listen, discern, and obey with clear hearts.

4. For the Brokenhearted

Comfort those crushed by disappointment. Heal swiftly. Restore joy. Renew their hope and rebuild their strength.

Corporate Decree — From the Quiet Place

We decree that the rhythm of grace governs this generation.

We declare that rest is the foundation of restoration.

From that rest:

- Healers rise
- Intercessors awaken
- Leaders soften
- Families mend
- and the Remnant rebuilds

A Personal Revelation — When Rest Becomes Worship

There was a moment when I had poured out to everyone else and had nothing left to give. As I sat in silence, the Holy Spirit whispered,

"Stop producing for Me and start being with Me."

That single sentence lifted a pressure I did not even realize I was carrying. In that moment, rest became worship.

Each time I chose to sit in His presence instead of solving another problem, I discovered that He could accomplish more in my stillness than I ever could in my strength.

Restored to Rest

Now that your heart has walked through release, renewal, realignment, rest, refill, repositioning, recommissioning, and recalibration, you stand in a new posture — **the posture of rest**.

There comes a moment in every healing journey when striving gives way to surrender, and surrender gives way to stillness. This is where restoration truly begins — not in doing, but in being. It is the moment when the noise fades, the tears settle, and the soul remembers how to breathe again.

As *Psalm 23:2–3* reminds us: *"He maketh me to lie down in green pastures: He leadeth me beside the still waters. He restoreth my soul."*

Resting in Him is not inactivity — it is intimacy. It is the sacred space where grace refines you and presence restores you. Here is the truth the Lord spoke to me that changed everything:

"Rest is the foundation to restoration."

Before there is renewal, there must be rest. Before there is rebuilding, there must be stillness.

In the quiet, God restores what words and warfare could not. He rebuilds your peace, redefines your identity, and renews your strength. This is not the rest of retreat, but the rest of recovery — where the battle-scarred are healed, and the weary find a new rhythm in His presence.

Prayer of the Restored Heart

Lord, teach my heart to carry peace without striving, to speak with clarity without anger, and to love with courage without fear.

Anchor me in stillness.

Quiet my spirit.

Settle my mind.

Let Your presence become my refuge and my rhythm.

Mantle me with wisdom.

Align me with grace.

And let rest become the foundation of everything I do. In Jesus' name, Amen.

Sealed in Peace

May your heart remain soft.

May your spirit remain steady.

May your life remain aligned with the rhythm of His rest.

May the peace of God wrap around you like a mantle.

May His stillness lead you.

May His presence anchor you.

And may His rest become the seal over your healing, your growth, and your next season.

You are restored.

You are renewed.

You are at rest.

PART III
Wisdom for the Restored Heart

Healing is not an event — it is a rhythm. It is the steady, quiet choosing of wholeness in places where brokenness once felt familiar. Now that your heart has been reset, realigned, and restored, you are stepping into a new way of living — one shaped by wisdom, not wounds.

This final section offers guidance for walking forward with clarity, peace, and spiritual maturity. It is not a mantle, not a ministry office, not a call to a title — just wisdom for any heart that has been restored.

These reflections are meant to steady you, to ground you, and to remind you of what healed living actually looks like.

1. Discernment Grows in Quiet Places

One of the first things I noticed after healing was how differently I listened. Clarity is rarely found in chaos. A restored heart senses differently — not from suspicion, but from sensitivity.

You notice when peace shifts.

You feel when a conversation tightens your chest.

You discern when old patterns attempt to return.

Quiet moments are where discernment matures. Return to stillness before responding. Wisdom grows in the pauses.

2. Every Relationship Does Not Belong in Your Restoration

This was one of the harder truths for me to accept. Healing does not require hostility — but it does require honesty. Some connections supported your brokenness, not your becoming. Some people only knew the unhealed version of you and will misunderstand the boundaries you now need.

You are allowed to grow without apologizing for the distance.

3. Peace Is a Daily Practice, Not a One-Time Experience

I learned quickly that peace didn't arrive once — it had to be chosen. Peace is not passive — it is protective. It guards your thoughts, your emotions, and your rhythms. A restored heart recognizes the difference between forced conversations and authentic ones, chaotic environments and aligned ones, draining commitments and divine assignments. Choose peace on purpose. It becomes the thermostat of your restored life.

4. Pay Attention to What No Longer Fits

After restoration, certain things simply stopped feeling normal. Healing stretches you. Restoration causes you to outgrow what once felt normal.

Your appetite changes.

Your language matures.

Your tolerance for confusion lowers.

Your desire for clarity increases.

Your boundaries strengthen.

Your sense of worth deepens.

What once drained you will feel too costly now. Pay attention to that. It is wisdom speaking.

5. Your Emotions Are Not Your Enemy — They Are Indicators

For a long time, I thought healing meant feeling less. I was wrong. A restored heart does not avoid emotion — it interprets it.

Anger may reveal a boundary crossed.

Sadness may expose a place still healing.

Frustration may point to misalignment.

Joy may confirm agreement with God.

Feeling deeply does not mean you have regressed. It means you are aware. Wisdom allows emotion to inform without permitting it to control.

6. The Power of Stillness

Stillness didn't come naturally to me — it had to be learned. Rest is the posture of those who trust God with outcomes. It is the language of surrendered hearts. When you rest, you are declaring: *"I believe He is working even when I am not."* I had to learn that my worth was not proven by productivity. Sometimes the most powerful warfare is stillness — not because you are doing nothing, but because you have chosen not to fight battles that belong to God.

In stillness, He resets your perspective.

He heals exhaustion that busyness has disguised.

He restores the sound of your voice, the rhythm of your peace, and the strength of your yes. Rest does not mean withdrawal — it means realignment.

It is where God quiets striving and teaches the soul to breathe again.

7. The Reward of Release

Letting go was not dramatic. It was quiet — and costly. When you finally let go — of people, pain, pressure, and pride — you discover that rest is not the absence of movement; it is the evidence of maturity.

It is the proof that you trust God enough to stop trying to be Him. Rest becomes the sound of healing fulfilled. You no longer have to defend your growth or prove your forgiveness. You simply live it — freely, fully, faithfully.

Check Your Heart Posture

- o Have I mistaken busyness for effectiveness?
- o Do I find it hard to rest without feeling guilty?
- o What does true rest look like for my soul in this season?
- o Have I invited God into my rest as much as I have into my work?

Ask the Holy Spirit to show you what rest looks like for you right now — not in theory, but in practice.

8. Protect the Clarity You Paid For

Healing demanded more from me than I expected — and I learned to guard it. Your healing cost you something — tears, honesty, surrender, discomfort, courage.

Protect what God restored.

Do not explain your peace to people committed to chaos.

Do not shrink your growth to make others comfortable.

Do not allow old triggers to decide new responses.

Do not return to what God delivered you from.

Wisdom guards what restoration gave you.

9. Live Light, Love Well, and Stay Aligned

This is the posture I now return to when life gets loud.

Your restored heart was not meant to be heavy.

Your healed life was not meant to be complicated.

Your new rhythm was not meant to be rushed.

Live lightly.

Love intentionally.

Stay aligned internally.

You did not come this far to return to who you were.

You came this far to become who you were always meant to be.

Let wisdom steady your steps.

Let peace govern your choices.

Let your restored heart lead your next season with grace, clarity, and courage.

You are ready.

CONTINUING THE WORK

The Pride of Unforgiveness opens the heart to what has been carried and unresolved. For many readers, that awareness invites a next step.

The Pride of Unforgiveness: An 8 - Day Pathway into Healing, Renewal, and Release was created to carry the heart work forward. It offers guided space for processing, prayer, and intentional response.

ALSO BY
TEMEILA C. DANIEL

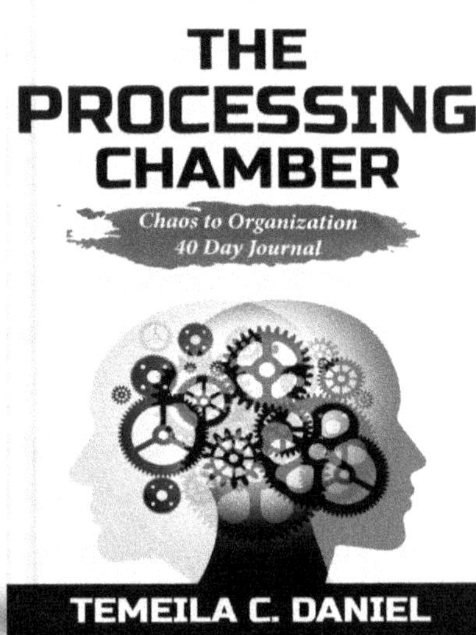

A Guide to Virtual
Meeting

Chaos to Organization
40 Day Journal

A Tool to Understanding and
Interpreting Your Dreams

CONTINUE THE JOURNEY

ELDER TEMEILA C. DANIEL

- TEACHING & MASTERCLASSES
- LEADERSHIP WORSKSHOPS
- CHURCH & EVENT SPEAKING

CONNECT WITH ME

Where the Kingdom and the Marketplace Meet

TemeilaDaniel.com

CONCISE
PUBLISHING HOUSE

This work was stewarded under the Concise Publishing House imprint, a curated house committed to bringing purpose-driven manuscripts to publication with clarity, integrity, and care.

Publishing & Production
Book Design & Formatting
ISBN & Distribution Guidance
Author Support

www.ConcisePublishing.us

The Sustainable Transformation Pathway

The *Sustainable Transformation Pathway* is designed to produce lasting transformation for the reader while creating sustainable *authority, impact, and stewardship* for the author.

This pathway centers the reader's experience, guiding them beyond *information* into *integration.* It is *not built for momentary inspiration,* but for *measurable change —* *encouraging reflection, application, and forward movement* *that extends beyond the final page.*

When a work is aligned with the *Sustainable Transformation Pathway,* it is intentionally structured to *support growth that is lived, not just learned.*